JÖRG HENNIG, M D
JENNY-BETH SCHMITT

THE
HEALTH LOGBOOK

FOR CLASSIC CARS
AND THEIR DRIVERS

AF188058

I

Dedicated to my English friends who have always supported me in keeping my classic cars healthy.

Jörg Hennig, M D
Jenny-Beth Schmitt

The

Health Logbook

for Classic Cars
and their Drivers

FSC
www.fsc.org
MIX
Papier aus ver-
antwortungsvollen
Quellen
Paper from
responsible sources
FSC® C105338

© 2020 by Jörg Hennig M D, Jenny Schmitt
Oelde/Germany

Manufacturing and publishing:
BoD – Books on Demand, Norderstedt

2nd Edition 2020/2. englische Auflage 2020

**German edition: Bordbuch und Gesundheitspass:
Ein Jahresbuch für Oldtimer und Fahrer**

ISBN 978-3-75044-066-1

TRI-TRIMMING® is a registered Trademark

Cover photos (2): Singer Nine Sports (1934)

Introduction

As a classic car owner, you can lose track of all the data and events related to the cultural property to be cared for.

Maintenance, care, MOT and the fuels and oils and lubricants to be refueled ... which tire pressure and which additives and if any which ...

How do you keep an overview of the ongoing repairs and inspections?

And if you are the proud owner of a classic car collection, it will be all the more difficult ...

What else has to be done before the classic car can be used for trips and what before the winter break?

And then you place very different demands on a classic car logbook than of a company car logbook.

Doctors know that not only the classic car should be taken care of in this way, but also the health of the driver.

That is why a logbook was designed here, which is dedicated to the "health" of classic cars and their drivers. Preventive examinations and medical treatments as well as the movement of the vehicle owner are therefore planned and documented in this logbook as well.

In this way, drivers and their classic cars are to be kept "healthy".

The campaign „Gesund wie ein Oldtimer (As healthy as a Classic Car)" supports this idea and is particularly committed to the prevention and therapy of diseases through exercise and sports. "Resting is Rusting" applies to classic cars and their drivers.

We are always open and thankful for good suggestions for improvement. Please write to the authors at info@dr-hennig.de.

Accompanying information you can find here:
www.gesund-wie-ein-oldtimer.de
or on Facebook: fb.me/The.Health.Logbook

We wish the users of this special annual planner good health and many happy hours with their classic cars.

The Authors

Jörg Hennig, M D   **Jenny-Beth Schmitt**

CONTENTS

This Edition was created in Cooperation with

I. Driver

Health Pass and Movement Planner

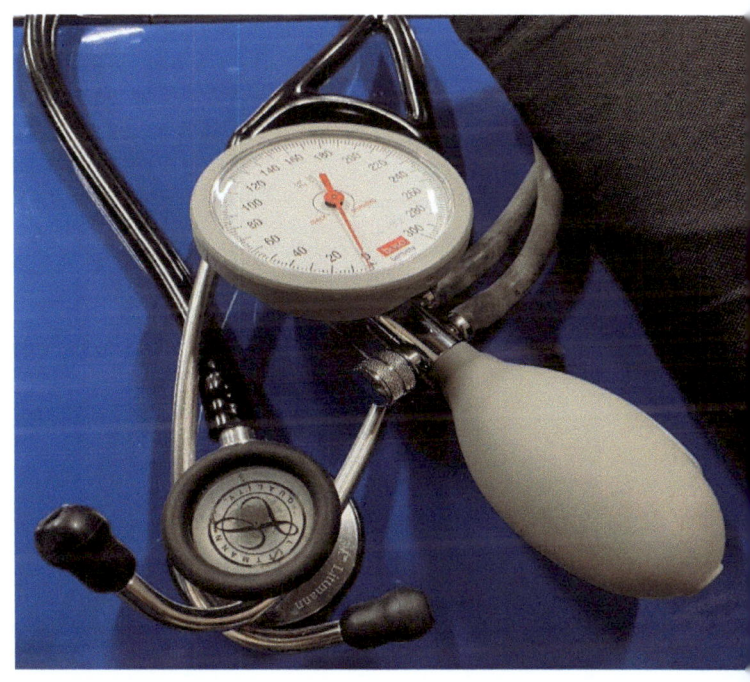

Vehicle owner data

surname	
first name	
date of birth	
health insurance	
address	

size (cm/inch)		
BMI*	25	30
weight (kg/lb)*		

*recommended

blood type	
allergies	

	√
organ donor card	
living will	

Treating Doctors

familiy doctor	
dentist	
emergency	NHS
999	111

Chronic Diseases	
o diabetes	o thyroid disease
o hypertension	o CHD
o heart failure	o lung disease
o stroke	o increased blood lipids
o operations	o cancer
o thrombosis	o abdominal disease
o others:	
o none	

Drugs plan

name/active substance	M	N	E

morning/noon/evening

Vehicle Owner Status at the Beginning of the Year

age	
height (cm/inch)	
weight (kg/lb)	
BMI	

last vaccinations	date
Td-Pert	
influenza/flu shot	

others	

last examination	date
general screening	
cancer screening	
prostate cancer screening	
breast cancer screening	
colon cancer screening	
skin cancer screening	
aortic aneurysm	
dental health	
vision test	
hearing test	
sports checkup	
driving license exam.	

Health Examination - „Great Inspection" for Drivers

!		√
	checkup/health examination	
	sports checkup	
	colon cancer screening	
	male cancer screening	
	prostate cancer screening	
	aortic aneurysm screening	
	female cancer screening	
	breast cancer screening	
	skin cancer screening	
	vaccination advice	
	travel vaccination advice	
	vision test	
	hearing test	
	dental health	

ANNUAL PLANNER / Important Appointments

JANUARY	
FEBRUARY	
MARCH	
APRIL	
MAY	
JUNE	

JULY	
AUGUST	
SEPTEMBER	
OCTOBER	
NOVEMBER	
DECEMBER	

To-Do-List

!	To-Do	√

!	To-Do	√

Doctor Visit/Hospitalization/...

date	doctor/disease/therapy

date	doctor/disease/therapy

Documentation of Self-Measurements (1/Month)

month	RR	pulse	BSL	weight	√
1					
2					
3					
4					
5					
6					
7					
8					
9					
10					
11					
12					

RR=blood pressure, BSL=blood sugar level

Documentation by Doctor (Quarterly)

	1.Q	2.Q	3.Q	4.Q
cholesterol				
HDL				
LDL				
triglycerides				
BSL				
HbA1c				
urine				
PSA				
RR				

RR=blood pressure, BSL=blood sugar level

TRI-Trimming ®-Logbook

week	swim	bike	run	√
1.				
2.				
3.				
4.				
5.				
6.				
7.				
8.				
9.				
10.				
11.				
12.				
13.				
14.				
15.				
16.				
17.				
18.				
19.				
20.				
21.				
22.				
23.				
24.				
25.				
26.				
27.				
28.				

week	swim	bike	run	√
29.				
30.				
31.				
32.				
33.				
34.				
35.				
36.				
37.				
38.				
39.				
40.				
41.				
42.				
43.				
44.				
45.				
46.				
47.				
48.				
49.				
50.				
51.				
52.				
53.				
target achieved				

Extensive daily documentation options in:
Hennig / Schmitt: TRI-Trimming®, see page 82

Resting is Rusting ...! - TRI-Trimming®

Tri-Trimming® is actually not a new sport, but Tri-Trimming® consists of the endurance sports of swimming, cycling and running.

It is well known in sports medicine that the combination of these three kind of sports and exercises is particularly beneficial for health. Due to the alternation of the movement patterns, sports damage or sports injuries occur less often even for beginners.

Tri-Trimming® for beginners involves performing a distance of a triathlon, completed in a week:
500 m swimming, 20 km cycling and 5 km running per week. It doesn't matter how you split it up.

Examples:
Monday to Friday 100 m swimming, 4 km cycling and 1 km running or daily
Monday swim 500 m, Wednesday 20 km cycling and Friday 5 km running or
Mon-Fri daily 500 m to the bakery and back, 2 km by bike to work and then back and swimming at the weekend 500 m or... or ... or ...

More informations: www.tri-trimming.de

26

II. Classic Car

Maintenance- and Logbook

Vehicle Data

manufacturer	
model/type	
year	
chassis number	
number plate	

engine oil*	

petrol (additiv)*	(yes/no)

coolant*	

tyre pressure*			PSI/BAR	
Front	max.		*	
rear	max.		*	

*recommended

Contact Persons

insurance
workshop
breakdown service
value reports
spare parts supplier

Vehicle Status at the Beginning of the Year

mileage	
date	mileage (km/miles)

last MOT	
date	mileage

last change of the engine oil	
date	mileage

new battery installed	
date	type

summer/ all-seasons tires		actually tread depth
production date	mileage	
F		
R		

summer/ all-seasons tires			actually
production date		mileage	tread depth
F			
R			

last lubrication service	
date	

last great inspection	
date	

last value reports	
date	condition/value

!		√
	first aid kit: check expiry date	
	warning triangle / vest: available?	
	parking disc: available?	
	tow rope / bar available?	
	reserve canister: available?	

ANNUAL PLANNER / IMPORTANT APPOINTMENTS

JANUARY	
FEBRUARY	
MARCH	
APRIL	
MAY	
JUNE	

JULY	
AUGUST	
SEPTEMBER	
OCTOBER	
NOVEMBER	
DECEMBER	

To-Do-List

!	To-Do	√

!	To-Do	√

Repair and Maintenance Work

date	workshop/repair/maintenance

date	workshop/repair/maintenance

Refuel Documentation

date	mileage	litre	add.	make	full

date	mileage	litre	add.	make	full

Consumption (l/100 km or mpg)

date	liters refueled / diff. mileage km		x100 = consumption/100km

Cleaning and Care

date	cleaning (inside/outside)

date	cleaning (inside/outside)

Great Inspection

(nach Oldtimer Markt Sonderheft Nr. 56, Seite 4)

!		√
	change engine oil and filter	
	change manual transmission oil	
	change automatic transmission oil	
	change rear axle gear oil	
	change power steering oil	
	check chassis bushings for play / cracks	
	check steering gear for attachment / play	
	check intermediate steering lever for play	
	rack and pinion steering: check cuffs	
	check / adjust clutch	
	check the suspension springs for breaks	
	check shock absorber for leaks	
	shock absorber wag test	
	check and adjust wheel bearings for play	
	lubricate the chassis completely	
	examine body and underbody	
	adjust the wiper arms	
	fill up splash water and adjust nozzles	
	check body seals for cracks	
	grease the door and main hinges	
	inspect gasoline hoses for cracks	
	sunroof: clean and grease rails	
	check the convertible roof for leaks	
	tires: Check condition and air pressure	
	pare wheel: Check condition and air pressure	
	lighting: check lamps	
	lighting: check reflectors	

	lighting: adjust headlights	
	first aid kit: check expiry date	
	warning triangle / vest: available?	
	parking disc: available?	
	towing rope/bar available?	
	reserve canister: available?	
	exhaust system: check suspension	
	check exhaust system for leaks and cracks	
	cardan shaft: check universal joints	
	cardan shaft: check hardy disc for cracks	
	set air filter flap to summer / winter	
	switch heating on or off centrally	
	test air conditioning and heating	
	check / replace radiator frost protection	
	check the cooling system for leaks	
	renew fuel filter	
	check spark plugs and replace if necessary	
	renew air filter element	
	check the V-belt tension, adjust if necessary	
	trailer coupling: spray in the socket	
	check and adjust the horn	
	battery: check acid density	
	battery: refill distilled water	
	battery: grease and cover the positive poles	
	alternator: check coals	
	check wiring harness for damage	
	seat belts: check function / condition	
	check the function of the indicator lights	
	change timing belt	
	check timing chain for wear	
	test brake fluid and change if necessary	
	bleed the brakes properly	

	refurbish the brakes	
	check disc brake pads, replace if necessary	
	adjust drum brakes, new pads if necessary	
	adjust the parking brake	
	adjust valves	
	ignition: change breaker contacts	
	ignition: adjust the closing angle	
	set ignition timing	
	carburettor / Injection: set idle CO	
	carburettor: adjust the float level	
	synchronize the carburettor	
	clean the carburettor	
	paint care (cleaning / polishing / waxing)	
	maintain and clean chrome/aluminum parts	
	clean rims	
	impregnate the convertible roof	
	vacuum the interior, ground maintenance	
	clean and maintain dashboard	
	clean and maintain wood	
	clean and maintain leather	
	clean and inspect windscreen/panes	
	clean and maintain seats	
	clean and grease seat rails	
	clean the engine compartment	
	clean the fuse box	
	clean the trunk/luggage space	

Checklist before Ride/Rally

	FIRST AID VEHICLE	
	torch; warninglight	
	towing rope/-bar	
	petrol canister	
	water canister	
	powerbank, jump starter, jumper cables	
	battery charger	
	kitchen roll, rag	
	duct tape	
	start pilot spray	
	cable ties, floral wire, hose clamps	
	light bulbs	
	radiator sealant	
	special tool kit fort he car	
	jack and wheel wrench	
	spare tyre	

	SPARE PARTS VEHICLE	
	2 fan belts (water pump/alternator)	
	fuses, relay	
	oil- and hydraulic fluid	
	sparks, -key, -cable/-plug	
	distributor cap, -contact	
	workshop-manual, spare parts catalogue	
	fuel hose	

	DRIVER AND CO-DRIVER	
	driving license	
	cash	
	comfortable clothing, gloves	
	comfortable shoes (tightly pedals)	
	sun glasses, cap, sun protection	
	travel proviant	
	travel pharmacy	
	smartphone charging cablel/adapter (12V)	

	VEHICLE DOCUMENTS	
	„The Health Logbook" ;)	
	operating manual	
	proof of insurance, service card	
	membership card automobile club	

	ORIENTATION	
	maps, navigation system	
	magnifier, reading glasses	
	writing utensils/blotting pad	
	stopwatch, odometer, radio clock	

	VEHICLE	
	antitheft devices	
	spare key	
	oil mat or painters fleece	

Logbook

date	
mileage before trip	
mileage after trip	
travel-distance	

predrive-check				
engine oil			coolant	
brake fluid			wiping water	
tire pressure			light	
horn			brakes	

logbook

special features

load battery			disconnect batt.	

date	
mileage before trip	
mileage after trip	
travel-distance	

predrive-check				
engine oil		coolant	
brake fluid		wiping water	
tire pressure		light	
horn		brakes	

logbook

special features

load battery			disconnect batt.	

date	
mileage before trip	
mileage after trip	
travel-distance	

predrive-check					
engine oil			coolant		
brake fluid			wiping water		
tire pressure			light		
horn			brakes		

logbook

special features

load battery			disconnect batt.	

date	
mileage before trip	
mileage after trip	
travel-distance	

predrive-check					
engine oil			coolant	
brake fluid			wiping water	
tire pressure			light	
horn			brakes	

logbook

special features

load battery			disconnect batt.	

date	
mileage before trip	
mileage after trip	
travel-distance	

predrive-check				
engine oil		coolant	
brake fluid		wiping water	
tire pressure		light	
horn		brakes	

logbook

special features

load battery			disconnect batt.	

date	
mileage before trip	
mileage after trip	
travel-distance	

predrive-check				
engine oil		coolant	
brake fluid		wiping water	
tire pressure		light	
horn		brakes	

logbook

special features

load battery			disconnect batt.	

date	
mileage before trip	
mileage after trip	
travel-distance	

predrive-check				
engine oil		coolant	
brake fluid		wiping water	
tire pressure		light	
horn		brakes	

logbook

special features

load battery			disconnect batt.	

date	
mileage before trip	
mileage after trip	
travel-distance	

predrive-check					
engine oil			coolant	
brake fluid			wiping water	
tire pressure			light	
horn			brakes	

logbook

special features

load battery			disconnect batt.	

date	
mileage before trip	
mileage after trip	
travel-distance	

predrive-check				
engine oil			coolant	
brake fluid			wiping water	
tire pressure			light	
horn			brakes	

logbook

special features

load battery			disconnect batt.	

date	
mileage before trip	
mileage after trip	
travel-distance	

predrive-check					
engine oil			coolant	
brake fluid			wiping water	
tire pressure			light	
horn			brakes	

logbook

special features

load battery			disconnect batt.	

date	
mileage before trip	
mileage after trip	
travel-distance	

predrive-check				
engine oil		coolant	
brake fluid		wiping water	
tire pressure		light	
horn		brakes	

logbook

special features

load battery		disconnect batt.	

date	
mileage before trip	
mileage after trip	
travel-distance	

predrive-check				
engine oil		coolant	
brake fluid		wiping water	
tire pressure		light	
horn		brakes	

logbook

special features

load battery			disconnect batt.	

date	
mileage before trip	
mileage after trip	
travel-distance	

predrive-check				
engine oil		coolant	
brake fluid		wiping water	
tire pressure		light	
horn		brakes	

logbook

special features

load battery		disconnect batt.	

date	
mileage before trip	
mileage after trip	
travel-distance	

predrive-check				
engine oil			coolant	
brake fluid			wiping water	
tire pressure			light	
horn			brakes	

logbook

special features

load battery			disconnect batt.	

date	
mileage before trip	
mileage after trip	
travel-distance	

predrive-check				
engine oil		coolant	
brake fluid		wiping water	
tire pressure		light	
horn		brakes	

logbook

special features

load battery		disconnect batt.	

date	
mileage before trip	
mileage after trip	
travel-distance	

predrive-check				
engine oil			coolant	
brake fluid			wiping water	
tire pressure			light	
horn			brakes	

logbook

special features

load battery			disconnect batt.	

date	
mileage before trip	
mileage after trip	
travel-distance	

predrive-check			
engine oil		coolant	
brake fluid		wiping water	
tire pressure		light	
horn		brakes	

logbook

special features

load battery			disconnect batt.	

date	
mileage before trip	
mileage after trip	
travel-distance	

predrive-check				
engine oil		coolant	
brake fluid		wiping water	
tire pressure		light	
horn		brakes	

logbook

special features

load battery		disconnect batt.	

date	
mileage before trip	
mileage after trip	
travel-distance	

predrive-check				
engine oil		coolant	
brake fluid		wiping water	
tire pressure		light	
horn		brakes	

logbook

special features

load battery		disconnect batt.	

date	
mileage before trip	
mileage after trip	
travel-distance	

predrive-check				
engine oil		coolant	
brake fluid		wiping water	
tire pressure		light	
horn		brakes	

logbook

special features

load battery			disconnect batt.	

date	
mileage before trip	
mileage after trip	
travel-distance	

predrive-check				
engine oil		coolant	
brake fluid		wiping water	
tire pressure		light	
horn		brakes	

logbook

special features

load battery		disconnect batt.	

date	
mileage before trip	
mileage after trip	
travel-distance	

predrive-check					
engine oil			coolant	
brake fluid			wiping water	
tire pressure			light	
horn			brakes	

logbook

special features

load battery			disconnect batt.	

date	
mileage before trip	
mileage after trip	
travel-distance	

predrive-check				
engine oil			coolant	
brake fluid			wiping water	
tire pressure			light	
horn			brakes	

logbook

special features

load battery			disconnect batt.	

date	
mileage before trip	
mileage after trip	
travel-distance	

predrive-check					
engine oil			coolant	
brake fluid			wiping water	
tire pressure			light	
horn			brakes	

logbook

special features

load battery		disconnect batt.	

date	
mileage before trip	
mileage after trip	
travel-distance	

predrive-check				
engine oil		coolant	
brake fluid		wiping water	
tire pressure		light	
horn		brakes	

logbook

special features

load battery			disconnect batt.	

date	
mileage before trip	
mileage after trip	
travel-distance	

predrive-check				
engine oil			coolant	
brake fluid			wiping water	
tire pressure			light	
horn			brakes	

logbook

special features

load battery			disconnect batt.	

date	
mileage before trip	
mileage after trip	
travel-distance	

predrive-check				
engine oil		coolant	
brake fluid		wiping water	
tire pressure		light	
horn		brakes	

logbook

special features

load battery		disconnect batt.	

date	
mileage before trip	
mileage after trip	
travel-distance	

predrive-check				
engine oil		coolant	
brake fluid		wiping water	
tire pressure		light	
horn		brakes	

logbook

special features

load battery			disconnect batt.	

date	
mileage before trip	
mileage after trip	
travel-distance	

predrive-check				
engine oil			coolant	
brake fluid			wiping water	
tire pressure			light	
horn			brakes	

logbook

special features

load battery			disconnect batt.	

date	
mileage before trip	
mileage after trip	
travel-distance	

predrive-check				
engine oil		coolant	
brake fluid		wiping water	
tire pressure		light	
horn		brakes	

logbook

special features

load battery			disconnect batt.	

Driven Events (rally/ride/...)

date	name of the event		kind

mileage before	mileage after	travel-distance

ranking	classification

remarks

date	name of the event		kind

mileage before	mileage after	travel-distance

ranking	classification

remarks

date	name of the event		kind

mileage before	mileage after	travel-distance

ranking	classification

remarks

date	name of the event		kind

mileage before	mileage after	travel-distance

ranking	classification

remarks

Hibernate the Car

!		√
	check / add coolant for antifreeze	
	fill up the fuel tank	
	battery: disconnect	
	battery: connect the maintenance charger	
	inflate tires to maximum air pressure	
	open the ventilation window slightly	
	do not apply the parking brake	
	remove loose floor coverings etc.	
	cover vehicle	

To-Do-List until Spring Awakening

!	To-Do	√
!	*obtain a new logbook*	

<u>Memo</u>

Jörg Hennig, M D

Specialist in general medicine, sports medicine, health promotion and prevention

Academic teacher at the Westphalian Wilhelms University in Münster/Germany
3. Chairman of the Sports Physicians Association of Westphalia

Jenny-Beth Schmitt

Medical assistant, Care assistant in the family practice, Non-medical practice assistant

Singer Nine Sports (1934)

The authors are interested in classic cars of all ages. They prefer to drive in pre-war classic cars and regularly take part in classic car rallies.

TRI-Trimming®

Motion is Medicine

Hennig, Dr. med. Jörg;
Schmitt, Jenny-Beth

ISBN 9783752877458, GERMAN EDITION
138 Seiten, 12x19 cm, Paperback
€ 11,90

Movement is medicine. That is why the author launched the TRI-Trimming® health campaign.
The book is designed in such a way that chronically ill people can manage the therapy of their illness with everyday movement and document progress.
Resting is Rusting ... TRI-Trimming® for a better Health

check4sports®

The sports check-up

Hennig, Dr. med. Jörg;
Schmitt, Jenny-Beth

ISBN 9783750461314; GERMAN EDITION
138 Seiten, 12x19 cm, Paperback
€ 8,90

A focus of sports medicine is prevention: newcomers and those returning to sports as well as experienced sports enthusiasts should definitely go to check4sports® to uncover risks and control training.
The aim of this book is to document these regular preventive examinations and the health status of the athlete over five years.

German language editions of all these booklets in this series

TRI-Trimming® - Bewegung ist Medizin
check4sports® - Die Sportvorsorgeuntersuchung
Bordbuch und Gesundheitspass – Ein Jahresbuch für Oldtimer und Fahrer
Hennig, Dr. med. Jörg/Schmitt, Jenny

The authors' series continues also as english editions.